Terra's Travel Guide for Kids:

Germany

By Anette E. Hillegass

Creative Consultant – Sabrina E. Hillegass

Ingram Content Group Inc.

La Vergne, TN

Anette E. Hillegass

Copyright © 2016 by Anette E. Hillegass

All rights reserved. No part of this publication may be reproduced, distributed or transmitted in any form or by any means, without prior written permission.

Printed by Ingram Publisher Services / Ingram Content Group Inc.

Book Design – Anette E. Hillegass
Creative Consultant – Sabrina E. Hillegass

Terra's Travel Guide for Kids: Germany/ Anette E. Hillegass. -- 1st ed.
Fun Around the World Book Series
ISBN 978-0-692-81058-3

DEDICATION

This book is dedicated to my husband John and my beautiful children
Sabrina, Natalie, and Rebecca.
Thank you for all your help and support –
I love all of you very much.

Additionally, a big thank you to my family and friends for their
constant support.

Contents

Chapter	Name	Page
1	Meet Terra	1
2	Location	2
3	Key Facts	4
4	Symbols	6
5	Highs, Lows, Middle	8
6	Let's Travel	10
7	Meet Kurt	12
8	Clothing	14
9	Etiquette	16
10	General Housing	18
11	Apartment Living	20
12	Pets	22
13	Wildlife	24
14	Grocery Shopping	26
15	Food	28
16	Meals	30
17	Recycling	32
18	School	34
19	Hobbies and Games	36
20	Famous People	38
21	Inventions	40
22	Art and Literature	42
23	Traditional Music	44
24	Holidays	46
25	Fun Facts	50
26	Cool Places to Visit	54
27	Activity Pages	90
28	Good Bye Germany	94

1 – Meet Terra

Hello, my name is Terra.

I live in the United States of America.
I love to visit my friends all over the world.
My friends teach me a lot about their culture and country that cannot be found in books.
Today, I will travel to Germany to visit my friend Kurt.

First, let's see what information I already know about Germany before we travel……

2 – Location

Germany's Official Name is:
Bundesrepublik Deutschland (Federal Republic of Germany)

Germany is located across the Atlantic Ocean in the center of Europe – it is one of the largest countries in Europe.

Germany borders nine other countries and two seas.

Countries bordering Germany are:
1. Austria
2. Belgium
3. Czech Republic
4. Denmark
5. France
6. Luxembourg
7. Netherlands
8. Poland
9. Switzerland

Seas bordering Germany are:
1. North Sea
2. Baltic Sea

Terra's Travel Guide for Kids: Germany

3 – Key Facts

Germany has an elected leader called Bundeskanzler (Chancellor).

The official language is High German (Hochdeutsch). There are as many as 250 distinct dialects used in Germany.

Germany's main capitol is located in Berlin.

Size: Germany is about 1,000 km (621 miles) long at its longest point (from north to south), and about 600km (373 miles) wide at its widest point. Germany is slightly smaller than Montana, USA.

Even though Germany is not that big, it is divided into 16 States:
Baden-Württemberg, Bayern (Bavaria), Berlin, Brandenburg, Bremen, Hamburg, Hessen (Hesse), Mecklenburg-Vorpommern (Western Pomerania), Niedersachsen (Lower Saxony), Nordrhein-Westfalen (North Rhine-Westphalia), Rheinland Pfalz (Rhineland-Palatinate), Saarland, Sachsen (Saxony), Sachsen-Anhalt (Saxony-Anhalt), Schleswig-Holstein, and Thüringen (Thuringia).

4 – Symbols

Each country has unique symbols for identification.

Germany's Country Symbols are:

1. **The German Flag** –the colors are black, red, and gold. The flag was first designed in 1832. The flag's colors are supposed to be a symbol of freedom and unity.

2. **Coat of Arms** –a black eagle against a yellow shield. The coat of arms is supposed to represent strength, courage, farsightedness and immortality.

3. **National Tree** – the Oak Tree. This tree is supposed to represent strength and endurance.

4. **National Anthem – Song of the Germans.** Das Lied der Deutschen/Deutschlandlied.

5. **Official Bird** – the Eagle. This bird is supposed to represent courage.

6. **Currency** – the Euro.

5 – Highs, Lows, Middle

Highs:
The highest location in Germany is a mountain called the "Zugspitze" (Windy Peak). It is about 2,963 meters (9,721 feet) tall. The Zugspitze is part of a mountain range called the Bavarian Alps. From the top of the Zugspitze, you can see mountaintops located in four different countries.
(Address: Eibsee-Seilbahn, Am Eibsee 6, 82491 Grainau, Garmisch-Partenkirchen)

Lows:
The lowest location in Germany is located in Neuendorf by Wilster. It is -3.50 meters (-11.5 feet) below sea level.
(Address: Neuendorf by Wilster, 25554 Steinburg, Schleswig-Holstein)

Middle:
The 'Mittelpunkt Deutschlands' (geographical center of Germany) is located in Thüringen. It has shifted several times during Germany's existence.
(Address: Mittelpunkt Deutschlands, Rothweg, 99986 Niederdorla, Thüringen)

Terra's Travel Guide for Kids: Germany

6 – Let's Travel

Now, that you have learned some facts about Germany, let's go and visit my friend Kurt who lives in Germany.

He will teach us about German culture, awesome places to visit, and some German fun facts.

First, we will need to buy airplane tickets, get our passports, pack our suitcases, and get to the airport.

We will need to fly by airplane from the USA to Germany. I live close to the Atlanta, Georgia airport and Kurt lives close to the Stuttgart, Germany airport.

It will take about 9 hours to fly over the Atlantic Ocean to our destination. The plane will leave Atlanta in the late afternoon and arrive in Stuttgart early in the morning.

I am so excited to fly – on the plane flight attendants serve meals and they have little TV's by each seat so I can watch movies and play games.

Let's go.....

7 – Meet Kurt

Here is my dear German friend Kurt – he will be your local guide.

Hallo everyone, my name is Kurt!
I have lived in Germany all my life with my mom Monica, my dad Andreas, and my little sister Ursula. As you can tell, our German names are a bit different from the names you are used to.

There are many things that are different over here. I hope you will have a wonderful time getting to know Germany – I have many interesting places I would like to show you.

Here is a list of some very traditional German names – and a picture of my family.

Do you have an unusual name – or a name that is very common in your country?

Traditional German Names:

Boys:	Girls:
Andreas	Heidi
Axel	Helga
Bruno	Ingrid
Conrad	Juliane
Ernst	Karin
Fritz	Liese
George	Martina
Peter	Petra
Roland	Tanja
Wolfgang	Ursula

8 – Clothing

German people wear modern clothing just like you. We pride ourselves on being fashionable and well-dressed.

On special occasions, like festivals and special holidays, we might wear traditional clothing which is called "Tracht".

Traditional clothing for women and girls is called a "Dirndl". It is a dress with a full skirt, a petticoat to be worn underneath, an apron, and a white blouse. The whole outfit is often embroidered with lace, ribbons and fine trim.

Traditional clothing for men and boys is called "Lederhosen". It consists of short, leather pants with suspenders and front flaps. These pants are worn with checkered shirts, a jacket made of coarse linen or wool, wool knee stockings, and a felt hat.
The "Tracht" will have different colors and slightly different looks depending which part of Germany you are at the time.

I never wear "Tracht" but some of my friends do – do you have special clothes where you come from?

9 – Etiquette

German people value order and etiquette. Here are some of our etiquette rules:
1. When introduced to a person, shake hands – no hugs (unless they are close friends or family).
2. When talking to a person, maintain eye contact so they know they have your full attention.
3. Do not address people by their first name unless they give you permission to do so first. Address them as Herr (Mister) or Frau (Misses) and their last name.
4. We like our personal space, so stay at an arm's length during daily interactions.
5. When you are invited for a meal, be on time – Germans are very punctual and consider even a small delay to be impolite.
6. Never eat with your fingers when you are invited to someone's house for a meal. Most Germans will even eat pizza and fries using a fork.
7. After a meal, place your knife and fork side by side to show that you are finished eating.

What are some of your etiquette rules?

Terra's Travel Guide for Kids: Germany

10 – General Housing

People in Germany live in various kinds of homes: some live in modern homes and some live in older homes that might have belonged to their family for generations.

In the countryside, people live in simple homes with land for farming. In the cities and surrounding areas, people live usually in apartments and row homes - single family homes are very expensive and many people cannot afford to buy one.

Many Germans try to live in towns and cities because it provides them easier access to jobs, stores, schools and entertainment.

My family lives in a row house in the outskirts of the city Stuttgart. We rent a 3 room apartment there: Living/dining room, my parent's bedroom, and the kid's room (the kitchen, bathroom, and hallway are standard and you do not count them as a room). Like most Germans, my family rents our apartment.

Where do you live?

11 – Apartment Living

Apartment living is very different compared to living in a house:
My sister and I need to play quietly because other families live below, above, and next to our apartment.

Our apartment is not that big, so I have to share a room with my sister. It gets pretty hectic in the mornings when we get ready for school and work, since we all need to share a bathroom – most apartments only have one bathroom. German bathrooms typically have only a bathtub in them - not a shower. All the rooms are not that big and we have no built-in closets here – you have to buy a 'Schrank' (closet/cabinet) instead. Our dining and living rooms are combined into one room.

Then there is "Kehrwoche", which literally means "Sweep Week". During "Kehrwoche" we have to clean the main staircase, the front walkway, the basement, and the attic. Once we are finished cleaning, we hang the little "Kehrwoche" sign on our neighbor's door.

How do you live? Do you have "Kehrwoche"?

12 – Pets

Germans love pets and have all kind of pets in their homes:

Dogs:

It can be very expensive to have a dog since there is a dog tax ('Hundesteuer') and very high veterinary costs. There are also many rules and regulations you need to follow when you own a dog. For example, in order to have a dog, you must ask your landlord for permission first. Dogs are allowed on trains, in restaurants, in banks, and many other places.

Cats:

Many Germans prefer cats since they are easier to take care of if you are living in an apartment. Also, there are less rules and regulations you need to follow.

Rodents, Birds, and other small pets:

Most Germans have small animals that can stay in a cage. My parents allowed us to have a hamster: Fluffball.
German pet stores have a huge variety of foods, treats, and toys for small animals since they are so popular.

Do you have any pets?

13 – Wildlife

Since Germany is located in the heart of Europe, we have a very nice variety of wild animals.

Depending where in Germany you are located at, you might see:

Deer, Quail, Pheasant, Chamois, Ibex, Wild Boar, Hare, Wildcat, Lynx, Elk, Wolf, Polecat, Marten, Hedgehog, Weasel, Porky Pine, Beaver, Badger, Otter, Salamander, Slow Worm, Lizard, Snake, White Stork, Fox, Red Squirrel, Pigeon, Mouflon, Marmot, Loon, Crane, and many more animals.

The best way to observe the wildlife in Germany is either to go for a walk or to ride a bicycle using one of the German trails. Many of our trails lead through fields and forests, or along waterways and mountains.

**Can you name all of our animals in the picture?
What kind of wild animals live in your country?**

Terra's Travel Guide for Kids: Germany

14 – Grocery Shopping

In Germany, we have small refrigerators in our apartments. Since we cannot store much food in them, we usually have to go shopping every other day. Most Germans will walk to a supermarket that is close by and purchase as much as they can carry.

When you arrive at the grocery store, you will need a one-euro coin for the shopping cart deposit. When you return the shopping cart, you get your coin back. Do not forget to bring your own shopping bags, or you will have to buy some at the store. The prices on the items already include all taxes, so you pay only the shown price. Also, at the checkout counter, you will need to bag your own groceries – it can be a challenge to try to keep up since most cashiers scan items really fast.

Stores are usually closed on Sundays because this day is considered a day of rest and a day for family and friends to spend time together.

Do you have a special routine when you go shopping? Is your shopping trip different from mine?

15 – Foods

Food has always been a major part of German culture. Germans tend to eat heavy and hearty meals that include big portions of meat and bread – the food preparations are very different in each German State.

We have a large variety of breads (over 300 types) and baked goods (over 1200 types of cakes and pastries), over 1,000 varieties of sausages, cheeses, and many other traditional foods.

Some German foods my family loves are:
Schnitzel (fried, breaded meat), Curry Wurst mit Pommes und Mayo (sausage with curry sauce and French fries with mayonnaise), Maultaschen (Swabian stuffed pasta), and Spaghettieis (vanilla ice cream with raspberry sauce).

Since we are located in the middle of Europe, we have many international fast food places – but I still love German food best.

What food do you like? Have you tried any German food?

16 – Meals

Germans have traditionally set meals:
Frühstück (Breakfast): We usually have some kind of warm drink like coffee (for my parents) or juice (for me and my sister), bread rolls, different kinds of deli meats and cheeses, boiled eggs, and some margarine.

Mittagessen (Lunch): We usually eat a heavy, hot meal that has some kind of meat with green vegetables and a side of French fries, or dumplings. Mittagessen is usually the largest meal of the day.

Kaffee und Kuchen (Coffee and Cake): Families and friends gather together in the mid-afternoon to drink coffee and eat cake. This time lets you relax during a busy day.

Abendessen (Dinner): We usually have a light dinner - bread, cold cuts, cheese, salads, or even leftovers from lunch. Our family always tries to eat our Dinner together so we can catch up on everyone's day.

What meals do you eat? Do you eat them with your family?

Terra's Travel Guide for Kids: Germany

17 – Recycling

Germans are very serious about recycling. My family recycles at home and I even have to recycle at school. We have several different colored bags for sorting trash in our kitchen:

Blue Bag is for paper and cardboard: All of your papers, boxes, magazines, newspapers go in there.

Yellow Bag is for plastic and metal: Plastic wrap, food cans, yoghurt cups, soap bottle, and old plastic toys go in there.

Brown Bag is for biodegradable waste: Leftover food, coffee filters, kitchen scraps, and tea bags go in there.

Gray Bag is for household waste that cannot be recycled: Light bulbs, diapers, photographs, and used tissues go in there.

Bottles and cans all go back to the grocery store's bottle machine for a deposit refund.

Do you recycle at home and at school?

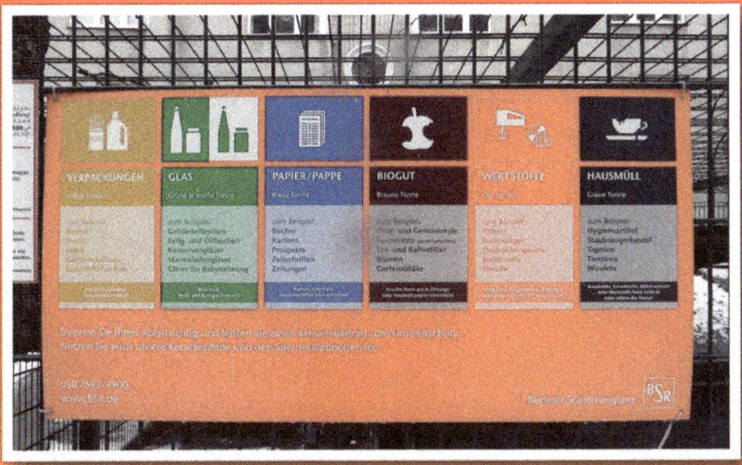
VERPACKUNGEN
GLAS
PAPIER/PAPPE
BIOGUT
WERTSTOFFE
HAUSMÜLL
Berliner Stadtreinigung

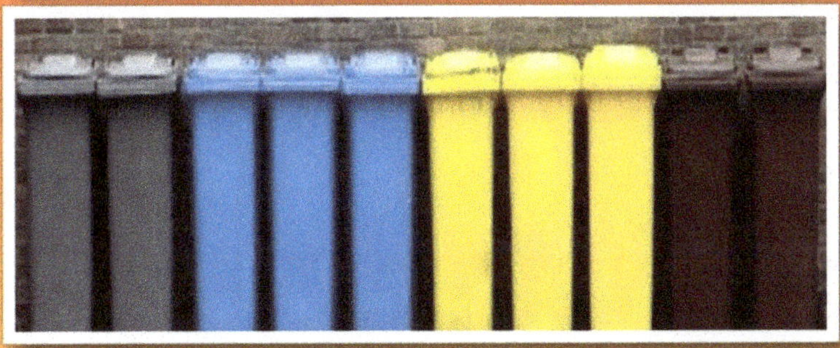

PFAND-
AUTOMAT!

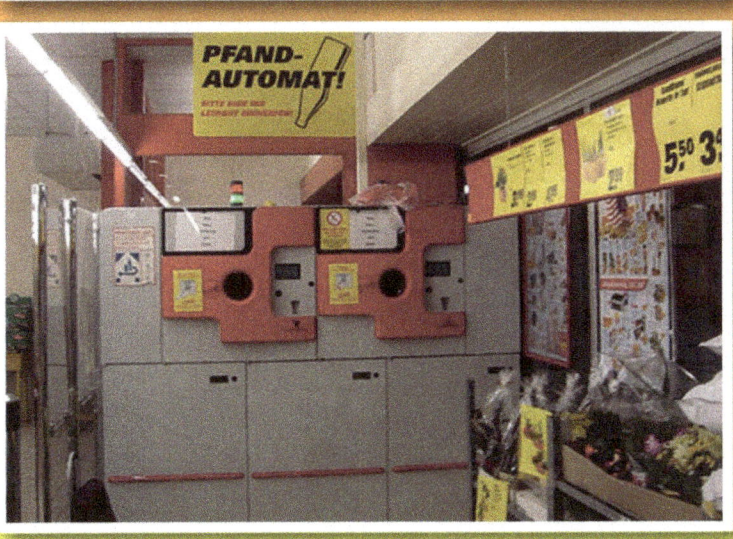

18 – School

School over here is very different: I have to take a public bus to school or I ride my bike to school, because we do not have school buses. My school starts at 7:45am and ends at 12:55pm. There is no cafeteria at my school, so I have to eat my lunch at home after school is over.

In German schools it is mandatory to learn English as a second language. Also, all children in Germany have to go to school, since 'Homeschooling' is not allowed. During summer, we have only 6 weeks of vacation. We have all our classes all year long – we do not have them divided into semesters.

My sister's friend just started 1st grade and she was super excited because on the 1st day of 1st grade she received her "Schultüte". The "Schultüte" is a large paper cone filled with toys, sweets, and school supplies. Entering first grade is a major step of growing up and the "Schultüte" is a symbol to celebrate the "'seriousness of Life". I would love to get one every year.

Is your school different? How do you get to school?

19 – Hobbies & Games

Family time is very important to Germans. My family usually spends evenings and weekends together

During our free time we love to do many different things: Playing soccer and ice hockey, hiking, camping, walking, biking, skiing, cycling, boating, rope climbing, snowboarding, swimming, traveling to other countries, visiting museums and zoos, listening to music, and reading books. We love being active outdoors whenever we find time.

During bad weather we also love to play different board games together. My favorite one is called: 'Mensch ärgere dich nicht'.

When I am not attending soccer practice, I love to spend some time with my friends at the playground. We love to play on the Zip line. Germany has many wonderful public playgrounds everywhere; we have 8 playgrounds close to my home.

What do you do in your free time?

Terra's Travel Guide for Kids: Germany

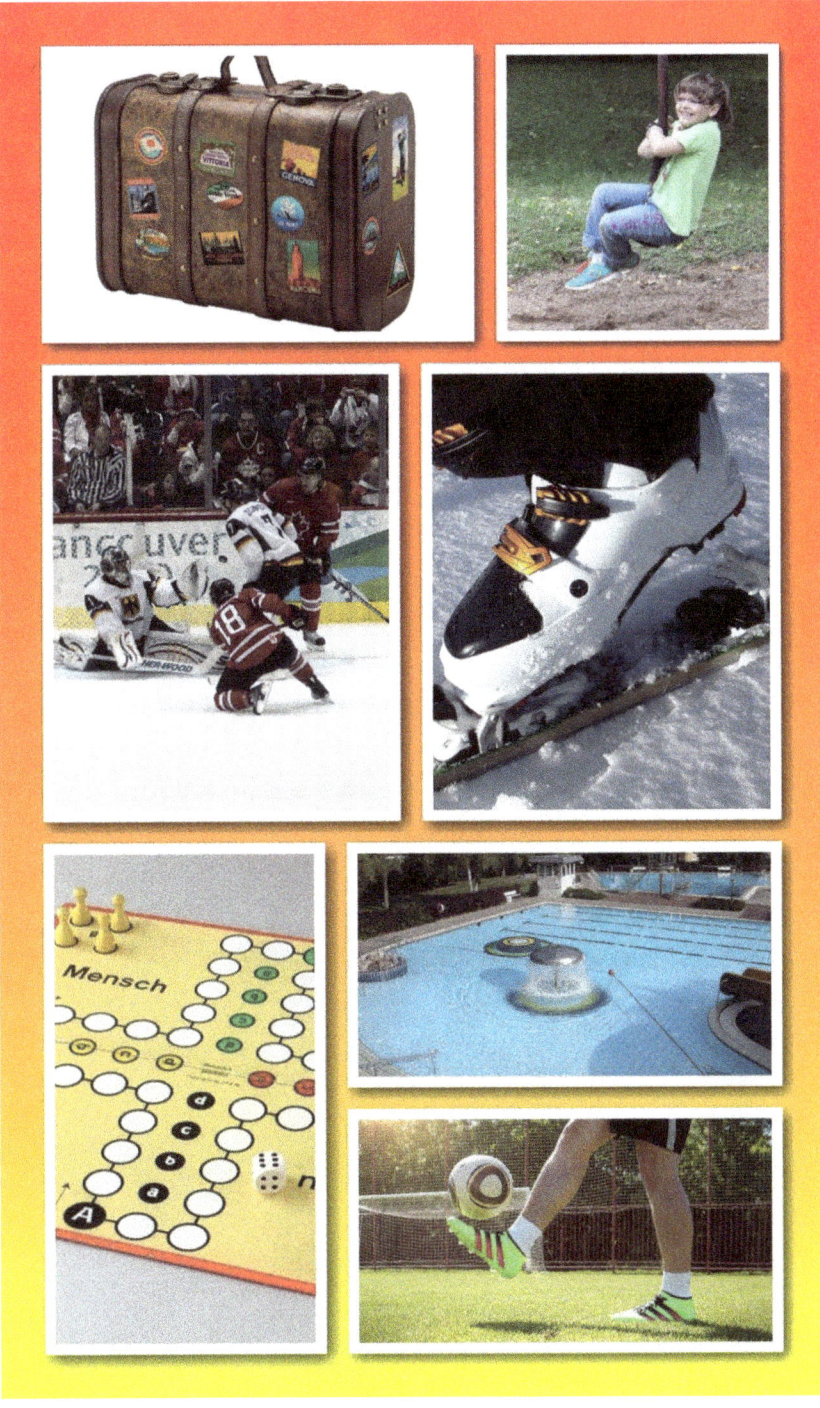

37

20 – Famous People

Germany is often called the "Land der Dichter und Denker" (Land of poets and thinkers). Germany's many famous people include great poets and writers, musical geniuses, inspiring composers, very intelligent scientists, innovative inventors, and wonderful painters.

Here are just a few famous Germans:
Johann Sebastian Bach, Ludwig van Beethoven, Johannes Brahms, Albrecht Dürer, Karlheinz Stockhausen, Friedrich Schiller, Thomas Mann, Karl May, Johann Wolfgang von Goethe, Caspar David Friedrich, Max Liebermann, Wihelm Leibl, Friedrich Schiller, Thomas Mann, Albert Einstein, Robert Koch, Felix Mendelssohn, Richard Wagner, Karl Benz, Rudolf Diesel, Robert Bosch, Albert Schweitzer, Wilhelm Conrad Röntgen, Konrad Duden, and many more.

Do any of these names sound familiar to you? Look at the pictures on the next page: can you match each name with the right picture?

I was able to match them all – after I had some help from my teacher!

21 – Inventions

German inventions have changed all of our lives. There are so many that it would take forever to tell you about all of them.

But just imagine not having any of these few German inventions around:
1. Automobile – invented by Gottlieb Daimler
2. Computer – invented by Konrad Zuse
3. Refrigerator – invented by Carl von Linde
4. Television – invented by Manfred von Ardenne
5. Book Printing – invented by Johannes Gutenberg
6. Bicycle – invented by Baron Karl von Drais
7. Video Games – invented by Ralph Baer
8. Clarinet – invented by Johann Christoph Denner
9. Toothpaste – invented by Ottomar von Mayenburg
10. Gummi Bears – invented by Hans Riegel

Additionally, the custom of the Christmas Tree and the Easter Bunny started in Germany too.

What exciting things have been invented in your country?

Terra's Travel Guide for Kids: Germany

41

22 – Art & Literature

Germans love art: There are actually more than 2,000 museums of all kinds in Germany
Wherever you go in Germany, you will also find plenty of theaters where you can watch plays and listen to operas.

Germans love Literature: Books are very important to our society; you can see many Germans reading wherever you go. Germany is one of the world's leading book nations - publishing around 94,000 titles every year. The first printed book was in German and the first magazine ever seen was started in Germany.

Here are a few German books that have been translated into English:
The Neverending Story by Michael Ende; The Little Witch by Otfried Preussler; Max and Moritz by Wilhelm Busch; Struwwelpeter (Fidgety Philip) by Heinrich Hoffmann; Inkheart by Cornelia Funke; Zamonia book series by Walter Moers; and Grimm's Fairy Tales by Brothers Grimm.

Go to your local library and see if you can find any of these books!

23 – Traditional Music

There are two very traditional types of German music that are very popular and well known:

Oom-pah Music: this type of music is part of "Volksmusik" (Music of the People) and is played at celebrations like Octoberfest and festivals The songs are usually performed using tubas and accordions and various other instruments.

Schlager Music: this is another popular style of "Volksmusik" that has been around for a very long time. Schlager songs are usually ballads about love and heartbreak. Schlager was the most popular during the 1960s and 1970s with very well-known singers like Rex Gildo, Peter Alexander, Heino and many more. These pictures show a few (of the many), very famous Schlager singers.

People either hate this music or love this music – there is no in-between: My mother and sister love Schlager, but my dad and I just wish it would go away.

Try to listen to some Schlager music on the internet – do you love it or do you just want it to go away?

Terra's Travel Guide for Kids: Germany

45

24 – Holidays

Germans celebrate many public holidays – here are a few:

February/March:
Karneval/Fasching (Carnival) – is a celebration with lots of parades including floats and people in fancy costumes with painted faces. The people on the floats throw candy into the crowd as they pass. Carnival comes from an ancient ritual marking the banishment of winter.

March/April:
Ostern (Easter) - the Easter celebration starts on a Thursday and ends on a Sunday. We decorate and paint hard-boiled chicken eggs. The 'Osterhase' (Easter Bunny) comes on Easter Sunday and hides colored Easter eggs for us kids to find.

September/October:
Oktoberfest – the first Oktoberfest started in October 1810, when Prince Ludwig and Princess Therese married and invited the whole town of Munich to the reception. All the people had so much fun that it turned into a yearly tradition.

24 – Holidays Continued

November 11:
St. Martin's Tag - this day is dedicated to St. Martin of Tours and celebrates modesty and selflessness. Days before this holiday, we start building our own lanterns and decorate them. In the evening of St. Martin's Day children have a lantern parade in towns and cities all over Germany.

December 6:
Nikolaustag: is the beginning of the Christmas season – the night before Nikolaustag, we leave our shoes outside the main door. If we have been good, we will find candy in our shoes in the morning. If we have been bad, St. Nikolaus and Knecht Ruprecht might show up and scary Knecht Ruprecht will give us a lecture on how to behave.

December 24:
Heiliger Abend (Hallowed Eve): for most Germans, this is the most important holiday - this is the night when the Christkindl (Christ Child) will come and leave presents under the tree. On this day, we have a celebration dinner with our loved ones and then we open our presents.

December 31/January 1:
Sylvester: the German New Year celebration – it begins on the last night of the old year. Sylvester is the biggest night for fireworks.

What holidays do you celebrate?

Terra's Travel Guide for Kids: Germany

25 – Fun Facts

I love to learn little 'Fun Facts' about different countries. Here are a few of Germany's fun facts:

1. We have nearly 700 zoological gardens, wildlife parks, aquariums, bird parks, animal reserves, safari parks, and 414 registered zoos (more than in the USA).
2. It is bad luck to wish someone a 'Happy Birthday' in advance.
3. The world's narrowest street is in Reutlingen and is 31cm (1 foot) wide at its narrowest point.
4. The longest word published in the German language is 79 letters long: Donaudampfschifffahrtselektrizitäten-hauptbetriebswerkbauunterbeamtengesellschaft.
5. Ulm Cathedral is the tallest church in the world, with 161.53 meters (530 feet) in height.
6. The Cologne Cathedral took 632 years to build and can hold over 40,000 people.
7. The world's two biggest cuckoo clocks are both located in Schonach in the Black Forest, Baden-Württemberg. One of the cuckoo clocks weighs 150kg (330 lbs.).

Terra's Travel Guide for Kids: Germany

25–Fun Facts Continued

8. The German Autobahn is the only Highway in Europe to have no general speed limit in most of its sections.
9. When President John F. Kennedy visited Berlin, he famously said "Ich bin ein Berliner", which can be translated into "I am a jelly donut".
10. When you go boating or swimming in the Bodensee (Lake Constance) you might end up in a different country. One part of the lake is located in Germany, another part is located in Austria, and another part is located in Switzerland.
11. Neuschwanstein Castle was used by theme parks and in Disney movies as the model for Cinderella's Castle.
12. German people are very straight forward and usually say exactly what they think.
13. One of the most unique places to stay overnight is in the Igloo Village located high up on the Zugspitze.
14. The 'World's Biggest Pet Store' is located in Duisburg, Germany. It has a selection of animals better than many zoos and stocks 250,000 individual animals of 3,000 different species.
15. The tradition of having and decorating a Christmas Tree comes from Germany.
16. In Germany the week starts on Monday and ends on Sunday.
17. Germany is the land of the Grimm fairytales.
18. The German alphabet has 30 letters.

Do you know any of your country's fun facts?

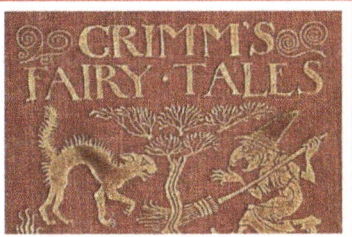

26 – Cool Places to Visit

Let me give you a tour of Germany and show you my favorite places in each of the 16 states:

1. Schleswig-Holstein
2. Hamburg
3. Niedersachsen (Lower Saxony)
4. Bremen
5. Nordrhein-Westfalen (North Rhine-Westphalia)
6. Hessen (Hesse)
7. Rheinland Pfalz (Rhineland-Palatinate)
8. Baden Württemberg
9. Bayern (Bavaria)
10. Saarland
11. Berlin
12. Brandenburg
13. Mecklenburg-Vorpommern (Western Pomerania)
14. Sachsen (Saxony)
15. Sachsen-Anhalt (Saxony-Anhalt)
16. Thüringen (Thuringia)

In each state, can you match the place to its picture?

Terra's Travel Guide for Kids: Germany

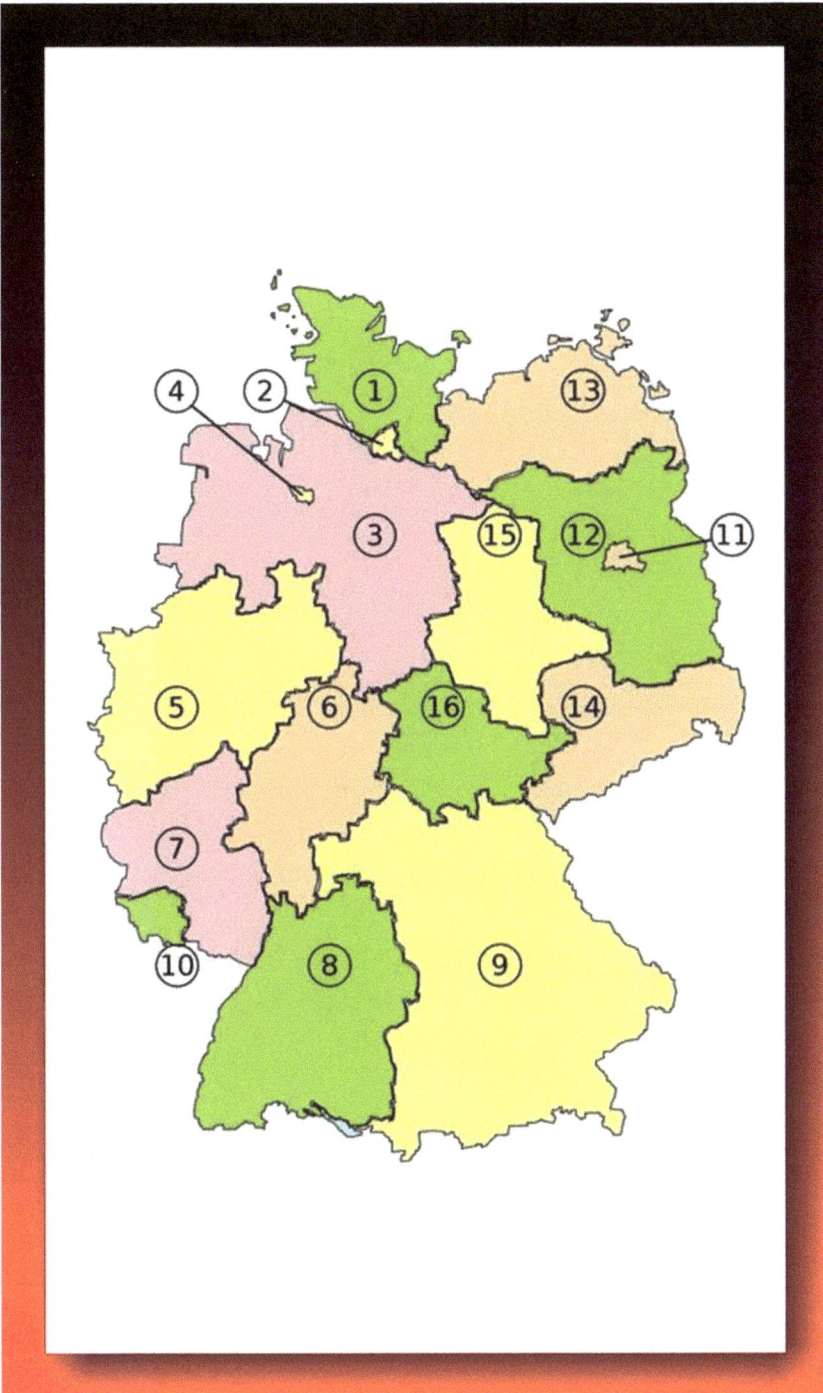

1 Schleswig Holstein

Goldnebel Electro Trikke Touren
This is the new way of sightseeing – on an E-Trikke. It looks like a 3 wheel scooter that is designed to make moving a lot of fun! Many people that have tried riding on one say it feels like you are skiing.
(Address: Willy-Brandt-Allee 10, 23554 Lübeck, Schleswig-Holstein   Web address: www.goldnebel-event.de)

Hanseschiff Lisa von Lubeck (Boat Tour)
This ship will make you think you are on an old pirate ship - it is an exciting tour. This ship is an actual replica (copy) of a 15th century ship.
(Address: Willy-Brandt-Allee 19, 23554 Lübeck, Schleswig-Holstein   Web address: www.hanseschiff-luebeck.de)

Meereszentrum Fehmarn
This is a wonderful aquarium with sharks and corals that can be viewed while going through an underwater tunnel. It has one of the biggest aquariums in all of Europe: it holds 3 million liters of water (about 800,000 gallons).
(Address: Gertrudenthaler Str.12, 23769 Fehmarn, Schleswig-Holstein   Web address: www.meereszentrum.de)

2 Hamburg

Bonscheladen
You have to come to this candy store if you want to see how candy is made. They even let you have free, delicious samples while you are there. This store has a huge variety of specialty candy.
(Address: Friedensallee 12, 22765 Hamburg
Web address: www.bonscheladen.de)

U-Boot Museum Hamburg
If you are claustrophobic, then this place is not for you: At this submarine museum you can actually go onboard a real Russian submarine. This is a B-515 Russian submarine that was built in 1976 and remained in active service until 2001.
(Address: St. Pauli Fischmarkt 10, 20359 Hamburg
Web address: www.u-434.de)

Miniatur Wunderland
Would you like to see many cities and towns of Germany within part of a day and walk through Austria, Switzerland, America, and Scandinavia right after? Then you have to come to the Miniature Wonderland in Hamburg.
(Address: Kehrwieder 2-4, Block D, 20457 Hamburg
Web address: www.miniatur-wunderland.de)

3 Niedersachsen

Filmtierpark

Would you like to pet and get to know some animal film stars? At the Film Animal Park, you can spend time with the animals and learn how they are trained.
(Address: Am Aschenberg 27, Höfer / Eschede, 29361 Celle, Lower Saxony   Web address: www.filmtierpark.de)

Snow Dome

Spring, summer, fall, or winter, you can go skiing or take skiing classes whenever you come here. Right outside the dome is a wave pool if you would rather make a splash in the water.
(Address: Horstfeldweg 9, 29646 Bispingen, Lower Saxony Web address: www.snow-dome.de)

Wattwagenfahrten zur Insel Neuwerk

If you love to play in mud and you love carriage rides then this is a 'must do'. Take a carriage ride to the small island of Neuwerk with its lighthouse. The whole, fun tour takes about 4 hours.
(Address: Wehrbergsweg 1, Ecke Duhner Strandstrasse, 27476 Duhnen, Cuxhaven, Lower Saxony
Web address: www.wattwagen-boldt.de)

4 Bremen

Schwarz Licht Hof

This place lets you play miniature golf under neon/black lights. To keep it even more entertaining, this place has some very unusual lanes. Make sure to wear a white shirt when you visit.
(Address: Cuxhavener Str.7, 28217 Bremen
Web address: www.schwarzlichthof.de)

Bremer Loch

The Bremer Hole looks like a manhole cover with a small coin slot in it. When you drop a coin in it, you will hear the sounds of the Bremen town musicians coming straight up from the ground: the donkey, dog, cat, and rooster
(Address: Am Markt, 28195 Bremen
Web address: www. bremen-tourismus.de/bremer-loch)

Universum Bremen

Not only does it look very cool from the outside, the Univerum is also an interactive museum with three floors of awesome attractions for children of any age on the inside. Expect to have lots of fun when you visit this place.
(Address: Wiener Str. 1a, 28359 Bremen
Web address: https://universum-bremen.de)

5 Nordrhein-Westfalen

Indoor Skydiving Bottrop

If you ever wanted to experience flying, then you should definitely come here. They will provide you with everything you will need - you will even receive a skydiving certificate once you finish your skydiving class.
(Address: Prosperstr. 297, 46238 Bottrop, North Rhine-Westphalia
Web address: www.indoor-skydiving.com/eng)

Aqua Magica

This is a wonderful place to go during summer time: it has a geyser, water pad, playgrounds and so much more. Do not forget to bring your swim clothes.
(Address: Bultestr., Bad Oeynhausen, North Rhine-Westphalia
Web address: www.aquamagica.de)

Irrland

This is the largest farm-adventure park in Europe. It has over 80 games, farm animals, exotic animals, water fun, huge slides, pools, and even a labyrinth.
(Address: Am Scheidweg 1, 47624 Twisteden, North Rhine-Westphalis   Web address: www irrland.de)

Terra's Travel Guide for Kids: Germany

6 Hessen

Kartbahn No Limit
This is a large indoor and outdoor Kart racing facility. They have two different sizes of race karts: Standard and Junior – so it is a great place at any age. I raced against my whole family – it was so much fun.
(Address: Frankfurter Str. 142, 36043 Fulda, Hesse
Web address: www.nolimitkartbahn.de)

Frankenstein Castle
Not the real Frankenstein Castle from the movies but this castle ruin is very interesting, the view is very cool, and the food at the restaurant is delicious. If you are really brave, you can take part in a scary dinner theater performance.
(Address: Nieder-Beerbach, Hesse
Web address: www Frankenstein-restaurant.de)

Edersee
This park is known for all the water activities you can do and wildlife you can see. The best part is walking on the humongous dam – definitely an incredible experience.
(Address: 34549 Waldeck, Hesse
Web address: www.edersee.de)

7 Rheinland-Pfalz

Rock Town
This place is great for climbing beginners and climbing experts. The climbing routes are changed every few weeks, so it never gets boring.
(Address: Kantstr. 38, 67663 Kaiserslautern, Rhineland-Palatinate
Web address: www.rocktown.eu)

Zoo Landau
A very unique zoo since you feel very close to the animals due to minimal fencing. Do not forget to bring your camera when you come to this wonderful zoo.
(Address: Hindenburgstr.12, 76829 Landau in the Pfalz, Rhineland-Palatinate
Web address: www. zoo-landau.de)

Barefusspfad
This barefoot path is about 4 km (2.5 miles) long and has many different walking terrains: grass, gravel, mud, sand, and even has a river crossing. Do not forget to bring food, drinks, and a blanket for a picnic afterwards.
(Address: Staudernheimer Str. 90, 55566 Bad Sobernheim, Rhineland-Palatinate
Web address: www barfusspark.info/parks/sobernheim.htm)

8 Baden-Württemberg

Wilhelma Zoo and Botanical Garden
This place used to belong to a king and it is absolutely incredible. It has over 1,000 species of animals and over 7,000 species of plants. There are many unique things to do: visit the butterfly enclosure (bats are in there too) or watch the sea lion show.
(Address: Wilhelma 13, Neckartalstr., 70376 Stuttgart, Baden-Württemberg   Web address: www.wilhelma.de)

Freizeitpark Traumland
This is a small, relaxing, and unique park. There are trampolines, pony rides, face painting, lots of candy, and much more. If you get too hot, just walk right next door to have a tour of the Bärenhöhle (Baer cave).
(Address: Auf the Bärenhöhle, 728020 Sonnenbühl, Baden-Württemberg
Web address: www.freizeitpark-traumland.de)

Stuttgart State Museum of Natural History
If you love dinosaurs then this place is perfect for you – it has the best collection of dinosaur models.
(Address: Rostenstein 1, 70191 Stuttgart, Baden-Württemberg
Web address: www naturkundemuseum-bw.de)

9 Bayern

Bavaria Filmstadt
This film studio has many props from popular German movies. Do you love the Neverending Story movie? Then take a ride on the dragon Falkor while you are there.
(Address: Bavariafilmplatz 7, Geiselgasteig, 82031 Munich, Bavaria   Web address: www.filmstadt.de)

Tucherland
This place is an indoor and outdoor playground jungle. It has trampolines, climbing castle, zip line, giant slide, and much more. It is a great place to visit all year round in any weather.
(Address: Marienbergstr. 102, Nürnberg, Bavaria
Web address: www.tucherland.de)

Salzbergwerk Berchtesgaden
Take a tour in a real salt mine: a train will take you into the mine, from there you get to slide down some steep miners' slides and walk through mine chambers. Do not forget a sweater and jacket since it is very cold down there.   *(Address: Bergwerkstr. 83, 83471 Berchtesgaden, Bavaria*
Web address: www.salzbergwerk.de)

Terra's Travel Guide for Kids: Germany

10 Saarland

Gondwana – Das Praehistorium
Dinosaurs are alive in this special museum with the help of electronics. 3D and 4D movies transport you right into the middle of this dinosaur world. You can also meet a 100 ton giant shark if you dare. Afterwards, play in the waterfall or volcano at their huge playground.
(Address: Bildstockstr., 66578 Schiffweiler, Saarland
Web address: www.gondwana-das-praehistorium.de)

Sarr Alpaka Gbr
This is a wonderful alpaca farm: stay overnight or stay for a few days and spend some time with real alpacas. You can take them for a walk in the woods, play with them, learn about them, feed them, and take pictures with them.
(Address: Im Almet 163, Erbeldinger Hof, 66119 Saarbrücken, Saarland   Web address: www.saar-alpaka.de)

Brennender Berg
This burning mountain has been on fire inside for over 300 years – when you get close, you can smell the fire and see spots of burnt earth on the outside - a very unusual and spooky mountain.
(Address: Schachtstr. 2, 66280 Sulzbach, Saarland
Web address: www brennenderberg.de)

Terra's Travel Guide for Kids: Germany

11 Berlin

Modellpark Berlin
If you want to see most of Berlin but do not have the time, then visit its smaller version. There are over 80 very detailed models that are definitely a must see. This place is located in a public park with a playground and is also the perfect location for a picnic.
(Address: Eichgestell 4, 12459 Berlin
Web address: www.modellparkberlin.de)

Ritter Sport Bunte Schokowelt
This is a huge shop of German chocolates in many flavors. They will even create your own flavor mix right there. For hands on fun, they even have a section where kids can make their own chocolate bars.
(Address: Französische Str. 24, Mitte, 10117 Berlin
Web address: www.ritter-sport.de/besuchen/berlin)

Game Science Center Berlin
If you are a gamer, this place is a must: it is small but has all the newest, futuristic game technology for you to try. I love their cool, out of this world, one of a kind sandbox.
(Address: Besselstr. 14, 10969 Berlin
Web address: www gamesciencecenter.de/en)

12 Brandenburg

Eismanufaktur Potsdam

This little place has 'out of this world', delicious ice-cream in regular flavors and some very unusual ones also. How about a spicy chili ice cream or dreamy Spaghettieis? Do not forget to get lots of whip cream, fudge and sprinkles with your ice cream.
(Address: Brandenburger Str.67, 14467 Potsdam, Brandenburg
Web address: www.eismanufaktur-potsdam.de)

Erlebnisbahn

Want to ride a Draisine (Railroad Hand Car)? This place has several different types to try out. This is one exciting way to go sightseeing and to get some extra exercise.
(Address: An den Wulzen 23, 15806 Zossen, Brandenburg
Web address: www.erlebnisbahn.de)

Biosphare Potsdam

Welcome to the jungle: This is a bio-dome with a rainforest and each hour a thunderstorm takes place inside it. This place has lots of exotic animals and even a butterfly house.
(Address: Georg-Hermann-Allee 99, 14469 Potsdam, Brandenburg
Web address: www biosphaere-potsdam.de)

13 Mecklenburg Vorpommern

Deutsches Meeresmuseum
This museum has absolutely all the information about sea life and fishing there is. They have many interesting exhibits, tropical fish, and also shark feeding and turtle feeding shows.
(Address: Katharinenberg 14, 18439 Stralsund, Mecklenburg-Vorpommern   Web address: www.meeresmuseum.de)

Rodelbahn & Affenwald Malchow GmbH
Enjoy an awesome toboggan ride followed by a walk in the Barbary Ape enclosure. The cool thing is that the apes are walking around free in the enclosure with you.
 (Address: Karower Chaussee6, 17213 Machow, Mecklenburg-Vorpommern
Web address: www.soomerrodelbahn-malchow.de)

Tauchgondel Zingst
It is an awesome experience to sink down into the ocean in this diving bell and see an underwater world.
(Address: An der Meiningenbrücke 1, 18374 Zingst, Mecklenburg-Vorpommern
Web address: www tauchgondel.de/tauchgondel-zingst.html)

14 Sachsen

Zoo der Minis
This zoo has only miniature animals. There are over 400 minis in this mini zoo – and some of them will be in the petting zoo section. These little munchkins are so adorable that you will want to take them all home.
(Address: Damaschkestr. 1, 08280 Aue, Saxony
Web address: www. zooderminis.de)

Irrgarten Kleinwelka
This unusual labyrinth is divided into three large labyrinths: The regular labyrinth, the adventure labyrinth, and the mystery labyrinth. Do not get lost, or you might just be here forever.
(Address: Am Saurierpark 2, Kleinwelka, 02625 Bautzen
Web address: www.irrgarten-kleinwelka.de)

Saurierpark
Here you can see giant dinosaur sculptures, play in the numerous dinosaur playgrounds, or dig in the sandpits for dinosaur bones and teeth. This park is very unusual and entertaining. I especially love the dinosaur seesaw!
(Address: Am Saurierpark 1, Kleinwelka, 02625 Bautzen
Web address: www saurierpark.de)

15 Sachsen-Anhalt

Halloren Schokoladenfabrik AG
Take a tour in this German chocolate factory: See how chocolate and pralines are made, visit the chocolate room that holds over 1.4 tons of chocolate art pieces, and sample chocolates along the way.
(Address: Delitzscher Straße 70, 06112 Halle, Sachsen-Anhalt
Web address: www.halloren.de)

Tote Täler an der Unstrut
This place is hard to find but it is worth the effort. Once you arrive you can watch real Koniks. The Konik or Polish primitive horse is a small horse, a kind of semi-wild pony from Poland. It is incredible to watch these wild horses.
(Address: Tote Täler, 06632 Freyburg, Sachsen-Anhalt
Web address: none available)

Seilbahnen Thale Erlebniswelt
This place is an entertainment paradise that has: chairlifts, gondolas, a 'Funny Island', a fun park, and the 'Witches Place'.
(Address: Goetheweg 1, 06502 Thale, Sachsen-Anhalt
Web address: www seilbahnen-thale.de)

16 Thüringen

Baumkronenpfad
This tree top path goes through several levels of the trees. Once you are above the forest canopy you have an amazing view. It is very exciting to take a walking tour this high up.
(Address: Nationalpark Hainich, Thiemsburg 1, 99947 Schönstedt, Thüringen
Web address: www. baumkronen-pfad.de)

Saalfelder Feengrotten
These colorful, fairy caves are very magical. There is also a little fairy park and a little fairy garden. If you are really focusing very hard, you might see some of the fairies that are hiding all over the place there.
(Address: Feengrottenweg 2, 07318 Saalfeld, Thüringen
Web address: www.feengrotten,de)

Explorata Mitmachwelt in Zella- Mehlis
This is a hands on place where you are invited to take part in over 80 science experiments. I actually want to use some of these experiments at the next science fair at my school.
(Address: Kirchstraße 1, 98544 Zella- Mehlis, Thüringen
Web address: www explorata.de)

Terra's Travel Guide for Kids: Germany

Fairy Tale Route

Deutsche Märchen Straße

The Fairy Tale Route is a 600 km (about 375 miles) long trip from Hanau to Bremen. It connects the towns and landscapes that were the inspiration for the fairy tales Rapunzel, Little Red Riding Hood, Sleeping Beauty, Cinderella, Hansel and Gretel, and many more.

In the 1800s, Jacob and Wilhelm Grimm travelled many times along this route. They listened to people tell fairy tales while they traveled together. The Brothers Grimm then printed books of the tales. Hanau is the start of the route which is the birthplace of the two Brothers Grimm; then the route goes over Steinau to their home where they grew up; and through all the cities where the Brothers Grimm studied and worked as well as regions which are linked to the fairy tales found in their Grimm stories, such as The Town Musicians of Bremen.

The whole route is marked with road signs depicting the heart-shaped head of a pretty, fairylike creature. It takes about 1 week by car to travel all of the route.
(Address: *Start: Hanau – End: Bremen*
Web address: www.deutsche-maechenstrasse.com)

Terra's Travel Guide for Kids: Germany

27 – Activity Pages

Let's have some German fun: Do some fun activities and learn some German!

Find your way from the USA to Germany:

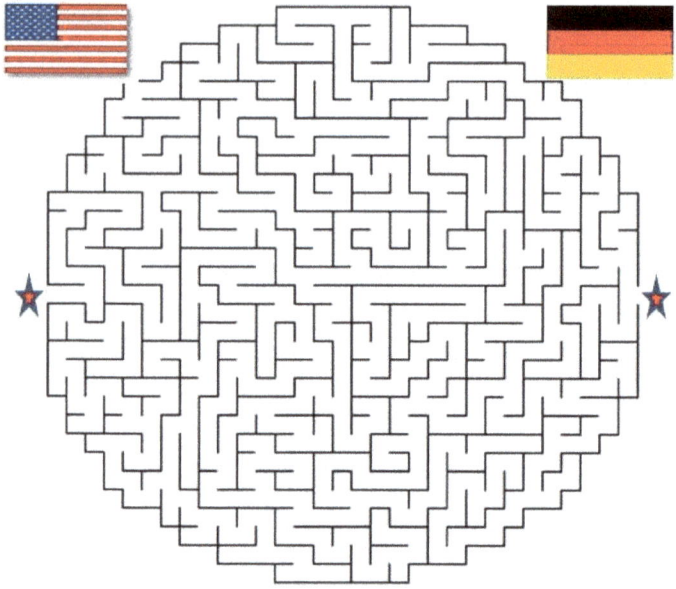

Terra's German Word Search

```
K D M L G V E D D O B B P H Z K O B
Z I V E A S I E I K L T O C U E J Y
U I A D U C N U R T A E M Q G G A E
G I D E T H S T N O U R M D S J B R
O V D R O N T S D B D R E C P F I C
E O E H B I E C L E F A S H I B T E
T D R O A T I H A R U P N G T E T I
H R K S H Z N L N F R R Q K Z R E N
E E U E N E O A K E I B E X E L I S
L I O N U L F N L S Z W E I K I M E
K G E L B J W D Q T K U R T S N M Y
N F S I L V E S T E R K I O R O T K
```

Find the following words in the puzzle.
Words are hidden → ↓ and ↘ .

ADDER
AUTOBAHN
BERLIN
BITTE
BLAU
DANKE
DEUTSCHLAND
DIRNDL

DREI
EINS
EINSTEIN
GELB
GOETHE
IBEX
KURT
LEDERHOSEN

OKTOBERFEST
POMMES
ROT
SCHNITZEL
SILVESTER
TERRA
ZUGSPITZE
ZWEI

German Numbers

English	German	Pronunciation
one	eins	(EYNS)
two	zwei	(TSVY)
three	drei	(DRY)
four	vier	(FEAR)
five	fünf	(FUENF)
six	sechs	(ZEKS)
seven	sieben	(ZEEBEN)
eight	acht	(AKT)
nine	neun	(NOIN)
ten	zehn	(TSEHN)

German Colors

English	German	Pronunciation
Black	Schwarz	(SHVAHRTS)
White	Weiß	(VIGHSS)
Red	Rot	(ROHT)
Blue	Blau	(BLOU)
Yellow	Gelb	(GELP)
Green	Grün	(GRUUN)
Purple	Lila	(LEE-LAH)
Brown	Braun	(BROWN)

German Words

English	German	Pronunciation
Hello	Hallo	(HA-low)
Good-Bye	Auf Wiedersehen	(owf VEE-der-zay-en)
Yes	Ja	(yah)
No	Nein	(nine)
Please	Bitte	(BIT-tuh)
Thank You	Danke	(DAHN-kah)
Friend	Freund	(froind)

Very Unusual German Words

1. **Ohrwurm (Ear Worm)**: having a song stuck in your head that you heard earlier.
2. **Fernweh (Distance Pain)**: the opposite of being homesick.
3. **Kummerspeck (Grief Bacon)**: the weight you put on when you "pig out" on food while you are upset.
4. **Purzelbaum (Tumble Tree)**: is a somersault on the ground.
5. **Zungenbrecher (Tongue Breaker)**: German equivalent to tongue twister.
6. **Luftschloss (Air Castle)**: an unrealistic dream/wish.
7. **Kopfkino (Head Cinema)**: Playing out a whole scenario in your head.

28 – Good Bye Germany

We hope you enjoyed travelling with us!!

I loved traveling to Germany and hope that you feel the same way after learning about Germany and its culture.

We left you your own travel list for Germany on the next page – fill it out and have it ready when you start your own adventure!

I will be visiting another friend in another country soon; why don't you come and join me on my next travel adventure? I would love to have you there with me!

Auf Wiedersehen!!!!

www.ingramcontent.com/pod-product-compliance
Lightning Source LLC
Chambersburg PA
CBHW040554010526
44110CB00054B/2690